A SIMPLE EXPLANATION OF CHURCH HISTORY

CONCORDIA PUBLISHING HOUSE · SAINT LOUIS

3558 S. Jefferson Ave.
St. Louis, MO 63118-3968
1-800-325-3040 • cph.org

Written by Molly Lackey

Manufactured in the United States of America

1 2 3 4 5 6 7 8 9 10 31 30 29 28 27 26 25 24 23 22

Our God works through history. He isn't just an ethereal being far above or an immaterial truth pervading all things. No—our God is Yahweh, the God of Abraham, Isaac, and Jacob. Our triune God—Father, Son, and Holy Spirit—not only upholds time and space but also joins us here in the midst of it all. That's why God walked with Adam and Eve in the garden, and Jesus was born of Mary, was crucified, died, and buried, and rose from the dead. God came into time to restore it, joined the human race to save it, and became a part of history to redeem it.

The Church—capitalized, meaning the universal and invisible collection of believers—has experienced both hardships and joys throughout history, each unique to that particular time and place. But in all times and all places through the protection of her Savior, the Church has been kept steadfast by the Holy Spirit, and she clings to Christ and His salvation.

This pamphlet looks at Church history broadly and from the unique vantage point of The Lutheran Church—Missouri Synod. For the purposes of this pamphlet, we have split the past two thousand years into seven divisions based on developments in Church history and therefore may differ from general American, European, or world history accounts. The divisions are meant to be a sort of map to help you navigate two millennia of fascinating—but complicated—history!

Our churches today face many opportunities and many struggles. May this brief history help you make sense of them all, past and present, and point you to your hope in Christ, who is both above time and in it, here with you, now and forever.

The Early Church (AD 30–500)

The beginning of the Christian Church is generally held to be at Pentecost, when the Holy Spirit came to the apostles. The apostles then proclaimed the Good News about Jesus to a crowd of people from all over the world. By the power of the Holy Spirit, the apostles preached the Gospel in the different foreign languages spoken by people in that crowd (Acts 2). The Book of Acts recounts some of the most important events of the earliest years of the Church: the death of the first martyr, Stephen; the conversion of arch-Pharisee Saul to apostle and martyr Paul; the first missionary journeys; and the persecution of the Church. The Epistles also give us a glimpse into the Early Church, especially the many doctrinal controversies that gripped the first congregations. The Early Church struggled with issues related to circumcision, diet, sex and marriage, Jew and Gentile converts, and antinomianism (the rejection of the role of the law and spiritual regeneration in the life of the Christian).

Rome distrusted "new" religions. Judaism was legal because it was an ancient religion; however, the Romans did not understand (or even care) that Jesus was the Messiah, the fulfillment of ancient prophecy. They thought Christianity was a new, invented cult. Further, since religion was a political matter, the Romans thought Christians were dangerous to the state. Civic religion—in which worship of the emperor was crucial—was the glue that held Roman society together, and anyone claiming an exclusive god was a danger to society.

The Roman government persecuted the Christian Church off and on until the early 300s with individual emperors expressing varying degrees of hostility. Large-scale persecution began under Emperor Nero (reigned AD 54–68) after fires destroyed nearly two-thirds of the city of Rome. According to the historian Tacitus, Nero blamed the Christians for the fires and began violent persecution as a way to distract and redirect public anger over the destruction, which many believed Nero himself had caused. Christians were an easy target because they were considered a "most mischievous superstition," and so Nero had them tortured and publicly murdered.[1] Public executions remained common in later rounds of persecution, including

1 Tacitus' *Annals* 15.44

the bloody Roman games at the Colosseum and elsewhere.

Persecution of the Church continued with sporadic pauses until Emperor Constantine (reigned 306–337). Constantine converted to Christianity and issued the Edict of Milan in 313, which made Christianity legal in the Roman Empire. Interestingly, Christianity became the state religion of Ethiopia around the same time; Ethiopians were among some of the earliest converts, including the eunuch whom Philip baptized (Acts 8:26–38). North Africa had a vibrant Christian Church: St. Augustine of Hippo was from modern-day Algeria and several early theologians came from Egypt, including Anthony the Hermit and Athanasius of Alexandria. These men are considered Church Fathers, early leaders of the Church who were central to its establishment and spread. The Church Fathers are not the same as the apostles. The apostles, such as Peter, John, and Paul, were those men who saw Jesus during His earthly ministry and proclaimed the Good News that He was God and had redeemed the world. *After* the apostles, the Church was led by men such as Augustine,

Justin Martyr, and John Chrysostom. Some, like Ignatius of Antioch, even knew and were taught by the apostles.

Also important to the Early Church were controversies, councils, and creeds. Divisions formed over issues like the divinity of Jesus and the nature of the Trinity. For example, Arius and his followers emphasized Jesus as subordinate to the Father to such an extent that it undermined His divinity. Arius was condemned as a heretic at the Council of Nicaea (which also produced the Nicene Creed). Other heretics arose, like Pelagius, who taught salvation by faith *plus* works. Augustine wrote against Pelagius and his teachings vociferously, reminding Christians that it was Christ *alone* who saved sinners. These divisions could have been destructive in the still-young Church, but the Holy Spirit raised up leaders and worked steadfast faith in them. The men whom God used to correct these errors were—and still are—an invaluable gift to the Church. The creeds and confessions they wrote are still used today to teach the faith and curb the erring.

The Early Church period was a tumultuous time of violence and change, controversy and conversion, new death and new life. We owe so much to the people of the Early Church: not only did they leave a treasure of doctrinal writings, they also converted many pagans to Christianity, proclaiming the Good News and clinging fast to their faith, even when it meant torture or death.

The Middle Ages (500–1500)

You know the saying: Rome wasn't built in a day. It didn't fall in a day, either. In fact, it took about a century for Rome to fall due to political corruption, moral decay, military impotence, and foreign invasion. Beginning in the late 300s, Germanic peoples known as the Goths flooded into the empire, slowly wearing Rome down through a series of wars, and by 476, a Germanic barbarian named Odoacer took the throne. Many historians consider this to be the end of the Roman Empire (the Western half, anyway; the Eastern half survived as the Byzantine Empire) and the beginning of the Dark Ages, also known as the Middle Ages or medieval period.

Despite the rather gloomy names historians apply to this period, it wasn't all bad. To be sure, life wasn't easy: the former Roman Empire was fraught with political instability, most people were impoverished and lacked rights we now take for granted, and disease, like the bubonic plague or Black Death, claimed millions of lives. Despite these hardships, the Christian Church grew during this period, especially among the so-called barbarians in northern Europe due to the vigorous activity of missionaries. Monasteries likewise grew, and it was within these monasteries that important Christian writings were maintained. Scribes copied the Bible and writings by the Church Fathers, ensuring that Christianity survived this tumultuous time. The faithfulness of the parishes that dotted the fragmented former Roman Empire kept the light of the Christian faith alive.

Meanwhile, trouble was brewing in the Christian Church. The first schism in Church history, known as the East-West Schism or the Great Schism, occurred in 1054 and rivaled the Reformation in importance. The Church on earth until this point had been one institution under the bishop of Rome, the office which eventually became the papacy. Churches in the east—Greece and the eastern Roman Empire, also known as Byzantium or Constantinople—bristled at the bishop of Rome claiming authority over the entire Church. These eastern churches also took issue with the phrase in the Nicene Creed: "The Holy Spirit . . . who proceeds from the Father *and the Son*"(emphasis added). They held that the Spirit proceeded from God the Father *only* and not from both the Father and the Son. While this may seem like a small difference, it was hugely important to the Medieval Church.

At the same time, changes sneaked into the Church that began slowly undermining the true Gospel. For example, the practice of selling indulgences developed out of the Crusades between 1100 and 1200. The Crusades were a complex series of wars that started when Christians living in and around Jerusalem appealed to the churches in Europe to defend them against invading Muslim forces. Over time, however, some lost sight of this original and just goal, and instead used war as a means to wealth and power. Indulgences were used to entice people to serve in the Crusades. Crusaders killed in battle were said to receive an indulgence, allowing them to skip purgatory and go straight to heaven. (In Roman Catholic teaching, purgatory is an intermediary place or state for Christians who die but have not paid the full temporal penalties for their sins.)

Acts of penance arose from the persecutions of the Early Church period, when some Christians denied their faith when threatened with torture and death. Later they repented and returned to the Church to seek forgiveness. In order to be reconciled with Christians who had suffered or lost loved ones to martyrdom, these people performed acts of penance. These acts were only intended to demonstrate the sincerity of their repentance, thus reconciling man to his brothers and sisters, not to God. But confusion crept in, and people began teaching that acts of penance (pilgrimages, special prayers, ascetic practices, and, later, serving in a Crusade) reconciled man to God, and Christ's death on the cross merely *made it possible* to please God through good works. This indulgence was initially given to those who donated money to the crusading effort, and it was only a matter of time before indulgences were sold outright.

Additionally, the Church began teaching that transubstantiation occurred during the Lord's Supper. *Transubstantiation* loosely means "the substance is transformed." It was thought the inner substance of the bread and wine were transformed into the body and blood of Christ. (While Lutherans believe that the Lord's Supper is Christ's body and blood in, with, and under the bread and wine, the Catholic Church has taught since the Middle Ages that they only *look* like bread and wine.) These Roman ideas about substances and appearances do not come from the Bible at all; they come from the writings of the ancient Greek (and pagan) philosopher Aristotle. While Aristotle's categories can be helpful in other settings, they are not helpful in theological issues because they apply a man-made, extrabiblical way of understanding things to God's revelation.

Because of such developments, reform movements sprang up in the late medieval period. Most notably the Czech theologian Jan Hus (1372–1415) taught that church services and the Bible should be available in the language of the people rather than in Latin, which most people could not understand. Hus was burned at the stake in 1415. His last words were prophetic: that though his executioners burned this goose (*Hus* means "goose" in Czech), in a hundred years, a swan would come whom they could not kill. Sure enough, 102 years later, in 1517, Martin Luther and his *Ninety-Five Theses* set off the Protestant Reformation.

While there were plenty of good things the Medieval Church maintained for future generations, the errors that developed during this period would lead to another important schism in Church history.

The Reformation (1500–1600)

The Reformation was a series of Christian reform movements that took place in Europe beginning October 31, 1517, when an Augustinian friar and university professor named Martin Luther (1483–1546) nailed a list of debate topics called *The Ninety-Five Theses* to the door of the prince's official church in Wittenberg, a backwater town in the state of Saxony. Dr. Luther meant to inspire a scholarly debate among his colleagues, but the common people got involved, and his theses were soon published and distributed across the Holy Roman Empire—especially throughout the German-speaking city-states and Austria.

Initially, Luther was concerned about indulgences, which he believed were being abused to fundraise and were undermining what it really meant to be a Christian: "The whole Christian life should be one of repentance" was Luther's first thesis. But he later criticized other aspects of medieval Christianity. For example, Luther argued that worship needed reforming; the priest did not re-sacrifice Jesus or perform a good work for himself or his congregation when he said Mass—beliefs that had developed during the Middle Ages—rather, God freely bestowed gifts onto clergy and laity alike in "God's service," also translated as "the divine service," to man. Additionally, Luther believed the pope was just a man, not Christ's vicar on earth, and thus was under the ultimate authority of the Bible. The Bible was also important for Luther, and he produced one of the most widely read Bible translations of all time. Not only was his translation written in the vernacular German, but also in clear, beautiful language so the Bible would come alive to the laity and they would better understand the freeing Gospel message.

Luther was fundamentally a conservative reformer, meaning he did not want to throw out the whole Roman Church and start over. Luther, in fact, did not intend to leave the Catholic Church at all; he wanted to stay and reform it from within, but he was excommunicated in 1521. Once it became clear that the Roman Church wanted nothing to do with Luther and his reforms, he distanced himself, calling his teaching "Evangelical-Catholic." However, it was the pejorative term the Catholics used that stuck—*Lutherische*, translated into English as "Lutheran."

Other reformers were not conservative like Luther. Some more radical individuals, like Andreas Karlstadt, claimed allegiance with Luther while advocating for complete overhaul of the liturgy and pastoral office. Others believed Luther did not go far enough. John Calvin thought that Luther did not fully break with the Catholic teaching on the Eucharist; Calvin taught instead that Christ was physically absent from the Supper and that the believer ascended spiritually to heaven. The Anabaptists went further still, rejecting infant baptism and insisting that only adult baptisms were valid. Luther soon found himself with foes on both the Protestant and Catholic sides; the Protestants sneered at him for not being a "true" evangelical, while the Catholics anathematized—damned to hell—him and all his followers at the Council of Trent (1545–1563).

Luther was not the sole creator of the Lutheran Church, however. His colleague Philip Melanchthon (1497–1560) was a monumental force and the author of the Augsburg Confession, a document written to explain the faith of the Lutheran princes of Germany. In 1580, a group of theologians, including Martin Chemnitz (1522–1586), known as the "Second Martin" for his influence on Lutheranism, compiled the Book of Concord, a collection of theological documents by Luther, Melanchthon, Chemnitz, and others that summed up the whole of the Lutheran faith. Five hundred years later, the

Book of Concord is still used by Lutheran churches as the definitive doctrinal standard.

The Reformation was not ultimately the story of Martin Luther. It is really all about Jesus: restoring Christ's rightful place in the Christian life, proclaiming His soul-saving Gospel into the ears of all people, pointing to His life-giving presence in the Sacraments. The Reformation began with the words "The whole Christian life should be one of repentance." Let us learn from the Reformation to daily return to Christ, our Lord and Savior, repenting of our sins and receiving His forgiveness, life, and salvation.

The Age of Orthodoxy (1600–1750)

The one hundred fifty years following the Reformation saw great achievements within the Church—and great divisions that would divide and endanger it for centuries. Within the Lutheran Church, this period is called the age of Lutheran Orthodoxy (*orthodoxy* simply means "correct teaching"), and it was a sort of renaissance for the Church. Other church bodies experienced similar periods of artistic and theological achievement;

the Catholic Baroque period, for example, saw an explosion of art and devotional material.

Some of the greatest Lutheran minds, writers, and artists lived during this time. The theologian Johann Gerhard (1582–1637) wrote a number of doctrinal and devotional works. His *Meditations on Divine Mercy* are a series of reflective, devotional prayers meant to drive the reader to examine his sin and cling to Christ all the more. Paul Gerhardt (1607–1676) was a pastor and hymn writer who wrote many beloved hymns still sung today. He is best known for "O Sacred Head, Now Wounded," which Johann Sebastian Bach (1685–1750), the most famous Lutheran composer, set to music. Bach produced a truly astounding life's work, more than one thousand musical compositions, including arrangements of the Passion of St. John and St. Matthew, more than two hundred cantatas, several settings of the Mass, and a huge collection of organ, harpsichord, orchestral, and chamber pieces, both sacred and secular.

Beyond the boundaries of Lutheran Orthodoxy, the rationalist movement was gaining influence over philosophy and theology. Rationalism developed alongside the Enlightenment, the philosophical movement that valued logic, reason, empirical knowledge (knowledge gained through the five senses: touch, sight, hearing, taste, and smell) and was skeptical about "irrational" knowledge, especially religion. The rationalism of the Enlightenment inspired civil upheaval across the world, including the American and French Revolutions.

One of the most famous Rationalist thinkers was René Descartes (1596–1650), a French philosopher who wrote the famous statement: "I think, therefore I am." While this may seem innocuous to us now, it was a monumental claim. Descartes was essentially saying that a person should doubt the existence of everything and anything outside of one's own mind. The statement led to the popularization of Deism, the belief in an impersonal god, and atheism, the belief in no god at all. Outside the Church, people grew skeptical, even hostile, toward Christianity. Within the Church, some began to downplay aspects of the faith as superfluous, distracting, or superstitious, like Jesus' miracles, the sacraments, and church art and music.

Then came the Romantic movement, which found Rationalism too cold and unfeeling. The Romantics were interested in nature, emotion, and the solitary man as a hero. Within the Church, the reaction against Rationalism was known as Pietism.

It is worth briefly differentiating between *piety* or *being pious* and *Pietism*. The first two are fine things for the Christian—one ought to strive to live piously, which simply means "devoutly" or "dutifully," and you may perform "acts of piety" that strengthen your faith and point you to Christ. These may include a regular devotional practice, crossing yourself in remembrance of your Baptism, and praying before meals or bedtime, among others. None of these things make you a better Christian, but such practices bring some people comfort and remind them of God's love.

Pietism, on the other hand, is the tendency to look to one's life—and the lives of others—in a legalistic way for proof of salvation. Pietism was especially strong within the Lutheran Church, and its adherents often claimed other Lutheran pastors and theologians overemphasized doctrine and underestimated the individual's life as a regenerated Christian. While it is certainly wrong to ignore the sanctification that goes on in one's everyday life, this accusation is often misleading or simply false.

While the Lutheran Orthodoxy was a golden age for the Lutheran Church, Rationalism and Pietism also threatened to distract the believer from Christ either by rationalizing Him away or focusing on works. Rather than trusting in our minds or our deeds, let us trust in Christ, borrowing Paul Gerhardt's words: "Lo, here I fall, my Savior! 'Tis I deserve Thy place; Look on me with Thy favor, And grant to me Thy grace" (*LSB* 450:3).

The Age of Revival (1750–1900)

The period between 1750 and 1900 covers a lot of ground; after all, it spans from before the American Revolution to fifty years after the Civil War. For the purposes of this pamphlet, we lump these years together as a period of Church history marked by revivalism. The final years of colonial America and the early years of the American republic coincided with the Great Awakening, an era of spiritual fervor including brash, emotive preaching and open-air revivals. Protestant churches experienced schisms such as the Methodist movement, an offshoot of Anglicanism, led by John Wesley (1703–1791). These splinter groups often gained popularity in America where state churches had less control than in Europe.

While there had been some Lutherans—specifically, a Pietist group known as Moravians—in America since colonial times, The Lutheran Church—Missouri Synod has its roots in a dramatic series of events in Germany and America in the early 1800s. In 1817, Frederick William III, king of the German territory of Prussia, announced that the state Lutheran and state Reformed churches would unite into a new Evangelical "Union" church. State churches had been the norm in Europe since the Reformation, and it made political sense (though not theological sense!) to merge. Reformed church leaders had long desired to unite with Lutherans, citing their closeness of belief, mutual opposition to Roman Catholic and radical Protestant dogmas, and respect for Luther. Lutherans resisted these efforts, pointing to the differences between Luther's and Calvin's understanding of the Lord's Supper and other issues.

This Prussian Union, as it was known, soon became a model of government-led church merging throughout the other German states. But as the unionization spread, so did opposition to it. In 1838 to 1839, a group of Lutherans who resisted attempts to unionize with the Calvinists left their homes in the state of Saxony—the same state where Luther had lived. The group, led by Martin Stephan, fled to America, eventually settling in Perry County, Missouri, about one hundred miles south of St. Louis. The early years were very difficult, and poverty and food scarcity were common. In spite of this, they set up churches and a school, including the one-room log cabin Concordia College. The college, founded by 19-year-old Carl Ferdinand Wilhelm Walther, became what is today Concordia Seminary in St. Louis.

Controversy arose within the colony in 1841 when it was discovered that their leader, Martin Stephan, was more interested in founding a cult of personality than a confessional church body. After Stephan was accused of adultery, the colony voted to depose and exile him. The power vacuum left the colony reeling, distraught over if they had erred—or sinned!—by leaving Germany and starting their own church. Were they even *Christians* anymore? In the midst of this turmoil, Walther assured the settlers that they were still faithful Christians, even if their original leader had misled them, because the Word of God was still among them. The colony voted to remain in Perry County under the leadership of Walther. In 1847, The Lutheran Church—Missouri Synod was formed, with C. F. W. Walther serving as its first president.

This period was marked by revivalism in broader Church history as well as in the Lutheran Church. The actions of the German government threatened to break down the Lutheran Church that so many had fought to establish and maintain over the centuries, but because of the revival of faithfulness (even in the face of persecution), transatlantic travel, poverty, and physical, emotional, and spiritual distress, the Lord sustained the truth of the Gospel through the Saxon Lutherans. Because of their bravery and faithfulness and the patience and mercy of our God, the Gospel was protected and passed on.

The Modern Church (1900–2000)

The world and the Church were rocked to their core by the bloodshed, genocide, famine, and wars of the twentieth century. The First World War brought about high casualties of young men and the crass destruction of western Europe, all because of an entangling series of treaties and an assassination by an obscure terrorist group. What followed this war was a brief interlude of moral license, rebellion against traditional Christian ways of thinking, and experimentation with new forms of government, namely, socialism in the new Soviet Union and fascism in Nazi Germany.

All too soon, Europe was plunged into another war, this time by the German dictator Adolf Hitler in his quest to overtake Europe and establish a totalitarian society based on a theory of racial superiority and antisemitism. Between the two world wars and the Holocaust, approximately one hundred million people died. Historians are less certain about the number of people killed by the

Soviet Union's political repression, gulags, prisons, famines, and mass starvations, but estimates range from twenty to over sixty million. In China, Mao Zedong's Great Leap Forward, an attempt to reorganize farmland under the communist system, led to the deaths of forty-five million people. In addition to war and oppressive governments, the early twentieth century saw the 1918 influenza pandemic, which some historians believe killed as many as 100 million people, as well as the U.S. stock market crash of 1929 and the Great Depression that followed, resulting in poverty and economic instability at a global scale. The Church and the world at large were reeling before they were even halfway through the century.

The Church's role in all of this is complex. In the early days of the First World War, many churches were supportive of the war effort, in large part because churches in Europe were state churches and thus closely associated with the government. In the 1930s and 1940s, Nazi ideology seeped into the German churches, resulting in "Positive Christianity," a theological movement that sought to promote Nazi racial purity through outrageous theological stances, like rejecting the "Jewish" Old Testament and claiming that Jesus was a Germanic Aryan, not a Jew. Meanwhile, communist countries grew exceptionally hostile to Christians, censoring clergy, spying on families, and arresting, torturing, and executing those suspected of resistance.

However, many people resisted violence and totalitarianism. In Germany, the Confessing Church, a group of clergymen opposed to the Nazification of Germany, committed to resisting the overreach of the government into the Church and to the fundamentally anti-Christian Nazi ideology in general. There were several prominent Lutheran pastors who resisted the Nazis, most notably Dietrich Bonhoeffer and Hermann Sasse. Later, Richard Wurmbrand, a Lutheran pastor from Romania, became one of the most famous missionaries and resistance leaders within the Soviet Union. Wurmbrand was repeatedly imprisoned and tortured, but he continued to preach the Good News of Christ crucified, even to his jailers. There are countless other men and women who likewise held fast to their faith in the face of violent persecution.

Meanwhile, trouble was brewing within American churches, including the LCMS, over the issue of biblical inerrancy. Some scholars in the 1930s and 1940s began questioning teachings in the Bible that were particularly hard to understand from a modern point of view, for example, Jonah living in the belly of a giant fish for three days or the virgin birth of Christ. But the issue did not end there: the death, resurrection, and substitutionary atonement of Christ also came under attack. By the 1960s and 1970s, there were reports of professors at Concordia Seminary in St. Louis teaching things about the Bible that were contrary to the confessions; some students said professors were undermining biblical inerrancy, while others reported that professors were going so far as to deny the resurrection of the dead. Tensions mounted between the seminary and the Synod, ultimately coming to a head with a walk-out by students and faculty on February 19, 1974. The group set up a Seminary in Exile, or Seminex. The students, professors, and parishes that sided with Seminex formed the Association of Evangelical Lutheran Churches (AELC) in 1976, which then joined other

Lutheran church bodies to form the Evangelical Lutheran Church in America (ELCA) in 1988.

Even as the Church was rocked by controversy and schism from within, it was being attacked from without. The culture was becoming increasingly hostile to the Church, especially on marriage and life issues. The sexual revolution of the sixties was followed by the legalization of abortion by Roe v. Wade in 1973, both of which attacked the Church's historic teachings.

Still, there was cause for rejoicing. Despite all of the darkness, division, and death that the twentieth century brought, the Church experienced unprecedented growth in places like Africa and East Asia. The light of Christ, undimmed by the horrors of totalitarianism, comforted the secret faithful in communist countries. And in our own context, despite the threat of harmful and erroneous teaching, The Lutheran Church—Missouri Synod withstood the shock of Seminex. The twentieth century was a difficult time for the Church, but God continued to show mercy.

Broader Christendom saw other major changes, like the nondenominational and seeker-sensitive movements, while many church bodies, including the LCMS, began encouraging increased engagement with the Bible and confessional documents, like the Book of Concord. In the culture at large, innovations like the personal computer and the Internet contributed to the rise of postmodernism, marked by a rejection of tradition, the rise of identity politics, and a deep skepticism toward institutions. These societal forces accelerated in the early twenty-first century, which so far has been rocked by terrorism, the decline of Christianity in the West, and the Covid-19 pandemic. But God continues to be unchangingly merciful, no matter what happens in the twenty-first century and beyond.

The End of History?

The Church today faces and will continue to face many of the same struggles she has faced throughout history. But these struggles will not last forever. History and even time itself will come to an end, when, as we confess in the Apostles' and Nicene Creeds, Jesus returns on the Last Day to judge the living and the dead. Those who rejected the forgiveness won by Christ will be cast out, but those who rested in the mercy of the Lord, from the Old Testament patriarchs to the faithful not yet born, will be ushered into everlasting life, freed from sin and death, in perfect union with God and with one another.

The end of history is coming—but that's good news! The end of history means the return of Christ and the glorious re-creation of the whole universe, fully reconciled to God and to itself. Be not afraid, dear reader, for your Savior returns, not to destroy time, but to bring its fulfillment! For in that day, Jesus "will wipe away every tear from their eyes, and death shall be no more, neither shall there be mourning, nor crying, nor pain anymore, for the former things have passed away" (Revelation 21:4).

May the peace of our God, who is the same yesterday, today, and forever, be with you. Amen.